Who Will Cradle Your Head

Poetry by

Jared Beloff

ELJ Editions, Ltd. is committed to publishing works of quality and integrity. In that spirit, we are proud to offer this poetry collection to our readers. Names, characters, places, and incidents either are the product of the author's imagination or are used fictitiously, and any resemblance to actual persons, living or dead, business establishments, events, or locales is entirely coincidental.

ISBN: 978-1-942004-52-3

Library of Congress Control Number: 2022951824

Cover Art by Scott Meskill
Cover Design by ELJ Editions, Ltd.

ELJ Editions, Ltd.
P.O. Box 815
Washingtonville, NY 10992

www.elj-editions.com

Praise for *Who Will Cradle Your Head*

In *Who Will Cradle Your Head*, Jared Beloff treats language with the same attentiveness with which he regards the Earth and its inhabitants—revealing a cradling consciousness, and the courage to love a dying world. The bird collector lays out the bodies of dead birds "in lines like ruffled silver, a tide of feathers." Deer "lift their black eyes from foraging," and "mustard grass and clover / spread like muslin over loss." In a remarkable sequence of poems, Sasquatch, the mythic human/animal hybrid, speaks with an instinctive intelligence, and from the lyric intensity of "our grief / which is also hope." These poems enact an acuity of tenderness that is rare in contemporary poetry. —Diane Seuss, author of *frank: sonnets*

In Jared Beloff's spectral book, the poet contemplates the enormity of climate change by noting the minute particulars of the natural world, and by shaping poems that square the fate of the planet with the life of the poet's own child who is invoked here with great tenderness, but whose fate must be imagined alongside our terrible knowledge of environmental catastrophe. *Who Will Cradle Your Head* is a book of hard truths, but it is also one that shows us how to conceive an alternate future in which Florida is under water, ice exists in museums, and Sasquatch sees the ocean for the first time. There are no easy consolations on offer--just the cool hand of poetry held to the warming world. —Mark Wunderlich, author of *The God of Nothingness*

In Jared Beloff's newest collection, *Who Will Cradle Your Head*, poems braid themselves between the environmental crisis, fatherhood, Sasquatch, and visual poems written for the eye and soul. These are poems that are tender *and* fierce, poems that look at the world around us and show how *reality whistles/in our faces*. The strength of this collection is how we seamlessly move from *last night's broadcast discussing climate anxiety/was interrupted by the magnolias dying outside* to Sasquatch seeing the ocean for the first time. Beloff is not afraid to play with poetry, to visually respond to *the world on fire around us* and to continue to make us want to turn the page. These insightful yet grounded poems make you think and feel, showing us the natural world and ourselves with both spirit and candor. —Kelli Russell Agodon, author of *Dialogues with Rising Tides* (Copper Canyon Press)

Jared Beloff is the closest thing I've ever encountered to a living, breathing shapeshifter. Like the Loup Garou, or Count Dracula, or Jacques Clouseau, he's willing to inhabit whatever shape or form or substance he needs to carry truth to us under the tightest of doorstops. Whether giving voice to Sasquatch, river birch, hamstrung politicians, or a father wishing a kind world for his daughter, the poems in Beloff's new collection, *Who Will Cradle Your Head*, are all driven by a single urgency to celebrate the value of this earth, of the air we breathe, of the people we love, and they are more than willing to try any possible angle to do so. Page by page, the poems move effortlessly from beautifully lineated verse, to prose blocks, to mechanical murmurations, and forms established by other poets. I simply cannot think of a recent collection more willing to explore voice and shape to get to what's necessary than this one, nor can I imagine a poet more capable of pulling it off than Beloff. —Jack B. Bedell, author of *Against the Woods' Dark Trunks*, Poet Laureate of Louisiana, 2017-2019

Jared Beloff's *Who Will Cradle Your Head* is a swirling tour of feral pigs who glow with radioactivity, a pensive and lonely Sasquatch, trees with human skin and weeping hair, and museum exhibits to disaster and sorrow. The world here is surreal, terrifying, gorgeous, and mournful—which is to say, the poems are true. They grapple honestly and starkly with extinction, grief, and adaption. Still, Beloff gives us the gift of insisting that even amidst disaster, there is art, there is love, there is joy—cracked and jagged-edged and hard-won and beautiful. —Teresa Dzieglewicz, author of *Something Small of How to See a River*

In the face of the climate crisis Jared Beloff's *Who Will Cradle Your Head* dazzles with its stark yet earnestly beautiful exploration of life and love and fatherhood. Beloff writes the way a soothsayer casts bones, and this book so powerfully renders the future it feels like poetry on the cusp of prophecy. I am awestruck, altered. "There is no earth / only soot and the animals retreating..." —Todd Dillard, author of *The Ways We Vanish*

For Zoe and Wren

Contents

Are All Your Predictions for the Future Real?

after Aimee Nezhukumatathil

If by real you mean as real as a house floating
into the sea, the waves claiming the kitchen,
sticker shock of a "For Rent" sign tacked to its side—
then *Yes*, every thought returns true, every line,
image, and imagination. I have dreamed them,
taken them from the night like a frown, so when
I speak in warning, I have weathered them all,
each siren's wail, a squall of hereafters. Can you
count the number of clear skies after a storm,
how many clouds rise like bouquets to meet us?
This one thins, another one bubbles, boiling
over as we flip through the news, "City Living,
With Less Water." Even now, reality whistles
in our faces, waits for light to shine each window's pane.

We don't think there's a positive ending…the most important thing
we can do for the future is to preserve as many of these species as
possible in museums, so that in 200, 300, or 500 years from now,
people will still be able to say this is what the Earth once had.
I strongly believe that.
-Robert Cowie

Everything changes;
Nothing perishes.
- Ovid, Metamorphosis

Animal Crackers

My daughter pulls animals out of the head of a large plastic bear like a magic trick, holds them up, asks, *What's this?* A large cat slopes its shoulders, front paw extended as if to find proper footing between her thumb and forefinger. We begin with names: *Snow leopard? Tiger?* The plastic bear's smile is wild. *Isn't this nice,* he seems to say, teeth tight with grit and grin, *isn't this sweet?* But then I remember the palm oil fires in Borneo, a cluster of orangutans pushed in a wheelbarrow, or the handful of bears emerging from the Russian Taiga's open maw, fur matted, gummed to a dull brown, come to rummage through the town's leftovers: wraps and rinds fished from metal dumpsters torn open like paper bags, need pushing us past margins of loss. *Giant panda. Sea otter.* Perhaps, the difference between accumulation and loss is a matter of proximity and scale, animals you can't fit in your palm, two dimensional as an endangered list. *Asian Elephant. Lowland Gorilla.* At what point do I stop her, tell her this is enough, knowing we will not be satisfied, that even our naming, since Adam, is an attempt to live in an unrecognizable world?

Watching Time Lapse Videos
with My Daughter

The sky pirouettes on a screen.
Several suns leap over a shadowed city,
cirrus clouds meet then scatter across stage,
a moon waggles in the wings. We don't blink.
Our pupils widen like sinkholes.

At this speed we are tail light thin,
reduced to ribbons and flares along the freeway.
We are raw scars of flame, a curtain of smoke swelling
to cover the wind's tapestry, pinions folded over loose
threads.

Her curiosity breaks our momentum:
When will we die? A forest glows in our hands.
The heave of Queen Anne's lace, a stand of sunflowers
stem their way through soil, stretch to their zenith,
turn their heads down as if to watch, as if to pray.
They look back over the earth they had left,
unable to remember the cause of their leaving.

The Ghost Forest

it is here we find the trees
with human skin. hair weeps
from their branches. when the wind blows
tendrils sway, a black river trailing through fingers.

river birches are peeling,
the silvered sides of their leaves speak
privately in the grove. a lake's surface
sits still, as tense as an open palm.

the cedars stand thin, broken and bare,
arms raised, twisting like antlers,
their sap traded for salt. a mockingbird
listens for a song, offers none.

when we breathe, the flesh moves,
drawing up to listen—what can we say
that would sustain, what story could hold them?
when we speak, the flesh puckers, afraid.

The Ship of Theseus

The ship they held in harbor
became a relic, a memorial
for honor or battle, remembered
a man whose name trembles
at the tooth's edge, trying to hold
a sound they could not keep:
each rotten board a tree,
each tree a root returning.

What is recognizable
is never certain: the way
a leaf breathes in light
or a wave will curl its undoing
back against the boards.
Each root a tendril tunneling
to find its proper ground.

Our taste buds change,
every seven years they shed
old favorites, find joy in new flavor:
tang of blood, sweat's brine
raising new questions:
how do we forgive the time
taken to forget ourselves?

A forest burns across continents,
a glacier calves cities of ice
which only just remember
they were once the ocean.
How long do we have
before we forget what we
have replaced: each nail
and tooth, the splinter's weeping?

Sasquatch mourns the pygmy rabbit

I walk the plains, tiptoeing the dark, heels yipped by a coyote's song. Loss rankles the bloodied mind. Your windblown carcass paws at the dirt under a star stitched sky laid bare. There are no signs of chase, nor torment—only bones stretching shadows in the soft light. Appetite, fear's push and pulse, tumbles like rivers just under the skin: after, we are never the same. My mouth is alive; need lifts my tongue, counts each tender ridge—I whisper these words for you my small friend, remembering the curve of your ears, your warm body shivering in the bowl of my hands. Silence will devour the mind if you let it. We were wise to keep our distance.

The feral pigs of Chernobyl are glowing

at night, fecund snouts move
through rubble, underbrush like pines
pushing up these thirty years,
to obscure each window's tilt,
widen each foundation's cracks:
the scent of decay holds
a greater half-life than any memory
we've made, pulls each bristle, crosses
each grind of tusk or tooth, keeps them
snuffling to prize and rust this solitude
we've buried, like truffles underneath
the average fungal bloom—
I imagine them pausing, looking up,
stars scattered like atoms,
feeling the cold air settling in
underneath their scentless luster.

Sasquatch ponders the seasons of decay

There are always signs of decay: a mite's wheedle through firs, the moss's sponge, fungus ringing the clotted soil. I've heard the dying trees sending their sap back out across the forest floor, seen cardinals bleeding out in the snow, cratered roots framing a burdened sky—I have witnessed the forest line pulling back, snow on the horizon's ridgeline less certain of its rest. What is left from fire will be doused in brine. In these years of twilight, I understand that to decay is to be unsettled in your return, each cycle a diminishment. Without a home, you are never lost, can never belong. When the last tree falls, will I be there to hear it?

Our Dreams of Late

after Layli Long Soldier

As we

watch   deny

the earth   the sky   the sea

tremble   flicker   endurance   expanse

we declare   we allow   we grapple   we wield   we forget

our grief   our grief   our grief   our grief   our grief   our grief

seeps   blooms   melts   flows   drowns

with voices   with love   with hatred   with silence

the past   the present   the future

unknown   remembered

dreams

The Bird Collector

Last summer's pulse nudged the tide, noticeable as salt graining the seawall. But the mangroves are pulling back, their roots like frayed brooms holding on to detritus. Spoonbills, gangly and roseate, have already left Biscayne Bay for higher ground. Somehow this hasn't been registered as a fact we can grieve. It is my job to collect the dead that circle Miami's mirrored light: Black-Throated Warblers lit by a night's shine, Northern Parulas searching out a distant home. Each bird crashes dreaming of a windowed horizon, not realizing the sea and its dotted green is already behind them. Everyone here is looking for more space and time. A group of warblers is called a confusion, spoonbills are called a bowl. I lay them out in lines like ruffled silver, a tide of feathers, a confusion of bodies, their mouths clattered open in search of food, a name lilting their small tongues. They stare out as if wondering which species is called a drawerful.

The Hall of Forgotten Scent

An empty room is shaped by a glass box
at its center. Inside, I expect lush green, breath

beaded surfaces. Instead, a yellow line
cuts the floor into revenants:

bodies placed, land claimed, withered and shed
like flowers found taped to browning pages,

brittle as summer grass cattle once roamed,
their stomachs churning cud.

Colors dream themselves miasmic upon a white wall.
A white blood cell spurts across my retina,

rides an iridescent breeze I cannot feel.
I am stopped by glass as pores open.

My feet swell, extending their roots through
a cratered floor to spread and loop some shape of me.

Mirrored below there is a reaching without name,
no plaque beside me, my hands leafing out, skin pulsing

with change. Above, hibiscus wavers on a hillside,
my inhalation slows to memory, each breath a taking.

Gasteranthus Extinctus

Last night's broadcast discussing climate anxiety
was interrupted by the magnolias dying outside,
shriveled pink, fried at the stems by frost.

A week of charred petals (sponsored
by some foundation's commitment
to build a *more verdant world*)

cling to green shoots the way a memory will stay:
my daughter picks blossoms from a fallen pear tree,
their translucent sequins against asphalt.

What is the name for death's expectancy?
Correspondents recall scientists naming flowers
for their extinction, a birthing sense of dread,

which reminds me to attend to death
before the dying, *Look Daddy*! But I don't
want to grieve for the planet anymore. Scientists,

new ones, rediscover thriving flowers untouched
by sprawl or the cancer in my father's veins,
a premature nostalgia.

Experiments with the Perception of Time

Scientists brought the bees underground frothing
to see if they could determine time's movement
leave the hive's geometry, return
to the humming order of a moment.
But what does it matter whether we are caught
in the angled slice of light, the ochre tint of home,
promise's syruped smell in a petri dish?
We feel earth's imperceptible arm toppling
on its axis, twitching with a drone's rhythm,
wind ringing our ears: each cell ruptured in song.
I watched you leave. Waited for you.
Routines cloying as coffee grounds, a stirring spoon.
I wanted to press down, still their clockwork, forget
each grain, sip only sweetness, clear as water.

A Maladaptation of Cells

adaptation · conditions · our risk

bees
will prepare
leave their hive
believing in fire. a
drone eats its body
weight in honeyed
mouthfuls limbs of
smoke billowing to
find home again
falling in
ashes

each
cell quiets
closed as smoke:
windows   blacked
an empty eye's tear
reveals the body's
dark shimmer each
silhouette. an eye
without light a
window
shut

Playing With Climate Models

Tonight, I'm hoping to catch the complexity of a curve refusing to touch its limit: the deep ocean seething, air wicking sweat from the soil's scrabble. What am I willing to admit? The line bends: straight as an ant's trusting scent given by the one who came before—who will mourn the last to follow as it lays down draping mold in the dirt? Nothing dies, only energy is given. Last night, I sat in the desert, heat written upon the rock's face. Even after dark, its beating seemed to breathe, to suggest my hand, if only gentle enough, could push through to its heart, hold its stillness, wanting to shift out of place. Everything changes, I know. Equilibrium greens each new reality, accepted like algae underneath sea ice. Energy is given, transferred. I run the scenarios again, play them like a scream trapped in a tree's rings.

Avoiding Maladaptation

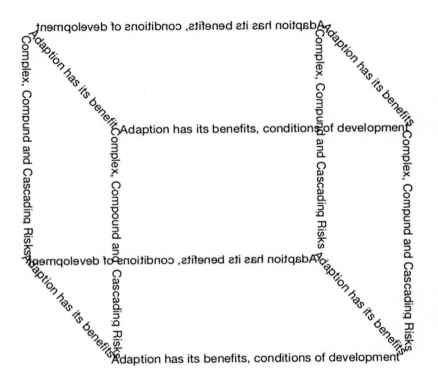

Exhibits in the Museum of Ice

A swan stretches her neck
before looping her bill, a bright shovel,
into the snow of her back.

The hall is bright, absent of sound.
Powder beneath our crampons
makes the floor sing. A door cracks
open on its hinges, crashes.

In another room, a man turns
a corkscrew into the ground
hand over hand, head tucked
down and away in shame.

We walk for hours holding hands
through thick mittens, the walls
bare, white. We listen for our hearts
beating like geese.

                There are tunnels
beneath us, wind wrinkles the surface,
snow serpents like water or a woman
waking to the sun's glare.

We enter a room rimmed by pots.
They fill and empty into the crisp air.
We are always moving. We don't know
when we began whispering names,

syllables escaping our mouths like fog,
spirits we hope would haunt us.

How to smile in front of a melting glacier

his jacket bunches at the knot,
wrists held in place before his
smile's rictus fades into the camera
light—he stands wondering
whether his lips now seep
through sand to rejoin the ocean
or the dark mountains revealed
beneath its gleam.

Sasquatch sees the ocean for the first time

My steps are clumsy in uneven snow, turning in puddled footprints, muddied between the mountain's folds. I am a disruption twitching on the ridge's flank until there is only water heaving, unsettled. I think of winter's hunger, the dark of a cavern's depth, deer halting in evening light to lift their black eyes from foraging. I am arrested as the water spreads, unhinges its jaw to swallow the land. Naked to the air, it calls like rocks falling, a crow's query. I blink back into the canopy, a jay pierces with warning, possessive and shrill, over answers it would deny.

The divers off the coast of New Florida

watch the Golden Girls as an archeological reality
before they close their eyes, splash over the bow:
imagine the water's rush sounds like an applause line;
their first breaths are canned laughter.

The bottom follows a grid: neighbor's lawns, faded
ellipses of a crosswalk. Mary peers out of her garden
grottos, her robes a billowed invertebrate, passive,
patient, forgiving each coral's miraculous growth
with an upturned palm.

Stilts bear each home, swell and root like mangroves,
each wall displays molded waterlines, a canyon's
black strata marks time: here when flooding stopped,
here the parabola that pushed Noah to collect cedar,

move to higher ground. A fin swats the water,
like a paper fan dismissing fantasy: the lanai is empty,
stares out into a blue that darkens without stars.
The divers listen to echoes, keep waiting for Betty
to quip *this is why we moved here* gesturing earnestly
at the vacant lot. Their laughter, at this depth,
only sounds like breathing.

Just another Tuesday in the Anthropocene

There's beauty in death if you learn how not to look for it. We talk about the weather in distant countries, sands shifting from one coastline to another. Here the sand is dredged, pumped from the edge of the continental shelf, fine and pure, hot on the pads of our children's feet. *Wear your sandals!* The wind lifts dust that has forgotten how to settle, coats our limbs in powder that glistens. *Look Dad, I'm a unicorn!* Our daughter holds her arms up sparkling, transformation on display. I try not to think too hard about the future she's growing into, how coral limbs will fan out one cell layer at a time, a thousand tiny polyps radiating in the warm sway before bleaching into mausoleums ground by acid and time, skin flaking in the sun, sifting to shimmer into sand. *Oh, what a gorgeous day.*

Freediving the North Star Academy Barrens

a faded pastel wall
bleached with coral and blue
waves breaking
impressions of ochre
stars, their chalky outlines wasting
the seafloor.

a kelp forest hangs
like streamers
from a party that has gone
too long, fish darting through
fronds that have no right to be here.

cracked paint calved,
scattered to the linoleum. in the detritus
an urchin's spike, an octopus' curled arm
blotched and bound by mold, foaming
through plaster tentacles,

reach to understand
blend billowed skin, retract
secrets in the frigid dark
like children probing a formless wash,
listening through broken shells.

Exhibits in the Archive of Sinking and Melting

Our boots are wet, the stamp and fray of pine needles
marking depth like endurance. It is still raining outside,
drops raking the pane litter the table with refracted life:
a set of keys to the abandoned home near the river's edge,
tickets to a flooded train, the spiked frame to a scientist's
boot, its blade dulled by each lift and fall, the rusted nail's
question bends with the wind.

What past are we preserving for the future
we would claim? My daughter points tarot cards
spilled from their deck: the queen of cups stares vacantly
at the carved whale bone both creased and chipped,
gathered, a foreshadow or a memory we wish to forget.

Drifting Further Everyday

We couldn't see him,
arms outstretched, a horizon
hidden by waves, haloed and drifting,

his skin dripping rust like light,
refracted. Too far, we thought hoping
every horizon folds to meet the next—

we couldn't fathom the surface,
each lapping wave, a nodding breath,
drifting further everyday.

Sasquatch returns to the coast

a day's light is wasted on me now, like runoff coating the skin. how long have I been standing here listening to the snarl of the sea? I feel the leviathan move: my stomach's churn, a weight that rests, a tail rattles at the throat. I wait for it to meet me, teeth pointed as spalled rooftops, prized and lashing at the heat's command.

Chirality

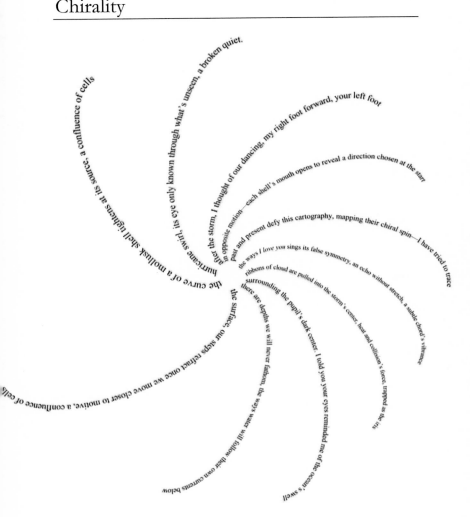

after the storm, I thought of our dancing, my right foot forward, your left foot

its eye only known through what's unseen, a broken quiet.

a confluence of cells

in opposite motion—each shell's mouth opens to reveal a direction chosen at the start

hurricane swirl, in streams at its source, a confluence of cells

the curve of a mollusk shell tightens at its source

past and present defy this cartography, mapping their chiral spin—I have tried to trace

the ways I love you sings its false symmetry, an echo without stretch, a subtle chord's vibrance

ribbons of cloud are pulled into the storm's center, heat and collision's force, trapped as its

surrounding the pupil's dark center, I told you your eyes reminded me of the ocean's swell

there are depths we will never fathom, the ways water will follow their own currents below

the surface, our steps retract once we move closer to motive, a confluence of cells

We paint the baby's room with Behr's
Melting Moment

and all we can do is wait for the thermometer's report.
Today its screen glows to reveal 76 degrees—somehow the
average body temperature has been decreasing; scientists
do not know why—it is mid-February and I have started
keeping watch over the blue of the hall's carpet, its frayed
edge spilling out across the threshold. My wife paints
clouds the color of permafrost as we approach wet bulb
temperatures halfway across the globe, learn to walk
through air cumulous thick—light chooses the afternoon's
swatch on the wall, penetrates ice undisturbed by the
scattered effect of air, a startled blue—I sit in the dark now,
listen for the sound of breathing, outside the stars' light is
too distant to reflect on the walls around us.

Eruption

You seem unconcerned: *it's happened
before.* An entire village unearthed

whole, petrified mid-sprint.
The harbor below spreads itself

to face the palette of the sky.
The mountain spews heat,

covers the sun, a smothered landscape
remaining like cinders twirling gray snow.

You bite into a peach's flame,
juice tearing the edge of your lip,

spilling something like anger, indifference.
Civilization, you begin to say,

until your mouth opens,
freeing a wall of smoke and ash.

The Earth is a Burning Haibun We Sing to Ourselves

after t.a. greathouse

once, you could search the air on any given Tuesday and your eyes would settle on the nearest cloud, formless and lonely, pulled at the ends like taffy or a marshmallow from a stave aflame before blowing out. once, we poured gasoline on our wounds, gouged our fingers in the dirt hoping we might sink and rot before we could wither. I asked your mother to dance with me one night as the sky glowed orange, street lamps winking like faerie lights. we went to bed sharing stories about your day, how your teeth had fallen out, how you held the white stones in your palm, a small river of blood wending through each valley and fold, your gapped smile a dark reminder of our growing.

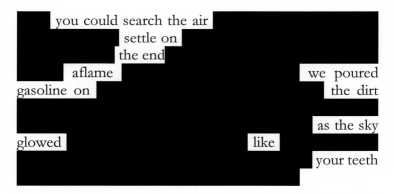

one night as the sky glowed orange,
we went to bed
held
your palm, a small river of blood wending
through each valley and fold

Politicians discussing climate change

faces, stripped like tree limbs,
                        or fish lipping
                        the water's skin
bald, scale sore and slow to rise,
                        or rocks that
                        hide beneath,
surfacing, determining the flow for
                        what we
                        cannot see:
an open mouth, a tongue caught
                        like a hook
                        speaking.
supplication sounds like drowning,
                        anger dips
                        under the ebb,
a ninth wave. we've run out
                        of names
                        for windswept
clouds and coasts battered
                        our arms
                        tired, tied.

Firstborn of the Dead

after Pablo Neruda

> *The sky vanished like a scroll*
> *rolling itself up, and every mountain*
> *and island was removed from its place.* - Revelation, 6:14

When the sky vanished, it was
all foreseen on the earth, parceled out,
maps marked in oil: ExxonMobil, Gazprom
British Petroleum, pipelines carving latitude,
dominion over the earth.

Along shifting coastlines, flies helixed over ships
forging new routes, past islands of dying trees
submerged dunes, silt ruddy with blood,
bleached coral like treasure or a burial of tombs,
homes sinking like rotten teeth on the floodplain:
a woman walks within boarded houses, seven Xs
across seven sealed doors, the river's flood thrashes
beyond the levies.

Meanwhile, an eye of fire ruptured in the Gulf,
a wall of flame replaces the West:
meanwhile, the Fruit Companies sprayed suntan lotion
on withered fruit, leaned on their worn bodies,
first generations picking cherries in the dark,
children cutting melons in the dark,
restless bodies rooted to the fields like windswept stalks.
And lo, they brought greatness and freedom and comfort
for the lowest prices packaged in plastic and cellophane,
their juices glimmering under the skin
in the market's fluorescent light.

Living Happily at the End of the World

after Ilya Kaminsky

The world ends like an almond tree pulled by its roots,
                withered brittle
                before it could rot.
A field sits fallow as a heat map
                angry pixels, clouds rising
                the color of ash.
A man with a loud tie mimes astonishment on TV:
                A deadly heat wave
                shattering all records,
as if weather were an adequate measure of pain.
                We live happily here,
                lying in bed, a fan
protests the heat of our bodies; we worry,
                but not enough.
                I am dreaming
of ice, an avocado, a bead sliding
                down a cocktail,
                there's an ache
ignored behind my eyes, water rising like a pulse,
                pressure then release.
                We sit up late and
speak of eucalyptus, the shape of convection,
                a kangaroo bursts
                through the underbrush.
I pass you a drink. We smile, the world on fire around us.

Tomorrow is Never

There is no heaven
only the haze we drape over ourselves.
We swell in our scaffolding, towers
reflecting each pleated thought.

There is no tide
only oil pluming across water.
We slick and dissipate, drifting
in the sun's overzealous spin.

There is no earth
only soot and the animals retreating; a doe
lays back down into the press of summer straw,
wary of the ark we never built.

Don't look back
for the dappled green, the startled bloom
of spring, hooked as we are—
tomorrow is never.

Sasquatch survives another fire season

The hollowed tree is an open mouth, a scream thinned by denial and time—in an empty pool all sound is a body floating, a song of fire ripples the surface. So much of what I want is closed like the fist of a seed, frayed as branches singeing themselves hollow. I walk past flared pine cones; listen closely, they speak of immolation's relief: here are the painted trillium blooms, here the rise of the underbrush, a blaze of blueberries flickering to life.

Adaptation

Restoration

after Ted Kooser

The rooms were vacant, says the broken glass
and tattered curtains in the farmhouse windows;
inviting too, says the burrowed length of the beds
in each drafty room; *and a good, well-loved home,*
say the pellets and peels next to the Bible torn
and broken below the window, brushed by sun;
but not for all, say the prints laid in the dirt,
leading to the door and the tall grass beyond.

*Desire is the slope down the back of hills
along the horizon,* says the glacier sliding
like a hand tracing each boulder freckled field.
Longing is the only measure of time, say the holes
tapped into the door's frame by searching birds
before a cold winter; *loneliness lays like snowfall
or the puddle's melt,* says the spray of mud left
at the narrow threshold.

Yet, something wrong is set right, say the roots
that buckle the boards. The fuzz of moss sugaring
pulp and dust says *there is nothing to return to;*
the cellar filled with dendrites—each splintered side,
every pipe spidered with rust, plow broken, the field
blossoming seed, an understory. Something set right.

Exhibits in the Museum of Dust

after Todd Dillard

All foreground is background,
a violence of tender voices.

The children have adapted. They swirl,
a mobius strip of arms outstretched,

catching lashes as they fall, their pockets full.
We shield our eyes, pretend there is still

separation. In a dark room, a man
continues to brush layers from his coat sleeves:

they smear like confection, palms shimmering,
diffracted gray with the scales of moth wings.

Down the hall, a woman weeps over a mound
of nail trimmings: she remembers only spiders

eating their mother, her blushing abdomen,
an orange web quivering.

In the last room there is an open window, a light
that fails to pin our spiraling bodies to the floor.

The possibility of grief

The problem is being human. Desperately seeking proof of life in the lay of an elephant's trunk, the nudge of a mother's foot against her child's cracked hide lying in drought, flies swirling helixes in the air. What should we make of her refusal to move, others who keep moving toward the horizon's dull shimmer? An elephant's foot contains muscles capable of interpreting vibrations through the ground. How do we measure the frequencies of our loss? Raised leg, pointed toe, a mother's nudge. Even though you have been gone for two years, my mind continues to stumble over your body, the quick pause of surprise, your mother's stubborn refusal to leave your side, lack of sound where your breath should be. When they find bones whose bleach they recognize as their own, a herd will stand in a circle together, faces gray, low moans vibrating syllables as sun and shadow, like a rib cage, expand.

Murmuration

Sasquatch salvages the edible ruins

Fire fuses tinder to the ash it must become: a ring of plastic cinched to the neck. Grain and gravel marrow to the sinew. I wade through foam, an edible ruin. This hunger hides bone, my skin the only organ left to gather history's fold, count each rib, measure its expanse against the pressure of the tide. What cannot be saved must change. What will not remain buried resurfaces in bloom.

In the fossil record, each layer speaks your name

for Erica

memory disappears in the swell
the tide's upheaval reaches out past regret,
exposed as ghosts—
here, our love is deposited for others,
revealed in the centuries passing,
gathered and hazing the horizon—
here, in our place in time,
I no longer remember
whether our words were spoken
or lay apart as stars ossified,
sounding against rock and air to say:
here and here and here.

The World Seed Bank

A
center
of stone
underwater,
forgotten, un-
reachable. Earth
moves and melts
compacted as time.
They wait—for the
first crack to open
to let the light
burn.

Sasquatch discovers an abandoned bunker

Stare hard enough and still edges will follow the lines of your eyes as you move away, a burst of color reveals absence in silhouette. A hatch lies open in a field of wildflowers, stalks candle thin, petals loosening—the bunker's vacancy echoes something forgotten. There are only shadows we would save, refugees from the storm's gray wall. We adjust to the darkness rimming a skull's sockets. An animal slept here, breathing in the murk, teeth scraping, a rasp against the quiet, its slow churn, a muscle's roil. Stare hard enough and you might see the stitches where softer pieces have knit together in black hollows where life once peered back.

Yayoi Kusama's *Pumpkin* washes out to sea

into undercurrent,
a mirror dulled
to white caps. The gourd
fills, empties the spray
it has been given—
an underside, squat and hollow,
cracks like a dropped shell
upon the ochre coast,
dotted sides winking
with each gust as if to say,
this is alright: *we must touch
our suffering to find the depths
of our joy.*

Sasquatch remembers places he has left

It's been six years since I left the green overtaking the dark trunk in a steady drip. Moss rivers itself in the cracked cambium I mistook for pith and youth reaching up to thread fingers through the draft. Below, the path is covered, removed, its tread and track faded. The stones sit cold remembering a time untouched by furrow or feeling, the slow union of lichen licking around an edge, hanging and frayed. I want to hold your small fingers, guide your smooth hand to trace the rock's ragged hem—my mind turns like clouds snagged in wind. Rain slips through a bed of needles, softens the crisis of footfall across the forest floor. Is the first tendril tunneling out from seed to feel the sand and silt of loam, a birth or a betrayal? A pebble in my hand, a jagged smile curved your face. I can feel the prick of catchweed and cleavers that have kept you. I imagine you happy here: snapping twigs, the neck of a red tanager's song.

Our Dreams of Love

after Layli Long Soldier

As we

mourn   recall

the earth   the sky   the sea

trembles   flickers   endures   adapts

we declare   we allow   we hold   we welcome   we realize

our love   our love   our love   our love   our love   our love

seeps   blooms   expands   flows   swells

with voices   with stillness   with song   with silence

the past   the present   the future

honored   repeated

dreams

Sasquatch explores Fresh Kills

This used to be landfill,
now wilding, overgrown, settling
        layer over composted layer
packing sediment, swaddling root,
        alive, intimate, suffocating—
the ivy's searching hands
        and bittersweet vines
swim the humid air
        filled with cicadas' static.
My foot hits an edge,
        a plastic thud, a doll's
mottled face, the remains
        of an abandoned car seat.
Who will cradle your head?
        What imprint will be left
as mustard grass and clover
        spread like muslin over loss?
I trace these green recesses
        like a scar's braided
renewal shading our grief,
        which is also hope,
a weave, which is memory
        but also love.

Revolution

reset the gene that lies dormant,
let your hand retract, reach away.
crawl with withered legs, belly gripping
back over the mess of leaves,
and trailing bodies to what we once were:
remember this sound? the earth's spinning,
blood's hammer and drum, the ocean's wash,
a withdrawal in your ear—turn back,
feel the slither and fin, shaking, resurgent.
let it rise up, teeming, primordial:
your lips curling around the call
naming what's undiscovered.

Sasquatch covers each footprint

Each tangle of birdsong above is like fear rising from moss and loam to loop each branch. I don't feel it anymore, suspended in this wind which mats my hair, cloaked in bramble and burr seeking to catch the skin. Don't be fooled, numbness belongs in the family of pain. I no longer know what genus I belong to, as if knowing were a way to choose. Begin listing taxonomies for how this is supposed to play out: an impossibility ignored until the myth falls upon edged rock, arches a trace in silt, rolling each print as a muddled fact waiting for witness. Always is what we tell ourselves in love and landscape, the promise of a clearing's light. I seek you there, held for a moment in the sun, aware that in our paralysis there is an ending.

Rewind

after Todd Dillard

cars inch in reverse along the freeway
careful not to tap the fenders behind them
free base their exhaust with a muffler's open straw
pull backwards into lots, driveways and dealerships.

our hands unshake, we let go: factory stacks
inhale smoke, a miasma of sparks spider back
to disassemble the front door, remove mirrors,
wheels, brakes, workers tear upholstery
like blisters until their arms hang limp

in the breakroom. derricks see-saw a slurry:
oil and mud, an unrefined plunge into the ground;
corn stalks replant whole, staked like golden flags
farmers wade out of their fields, their hands float
over grain, feel their callouses soften, their grip

loosens like seeds. jets vacuum white vapor
like Icarus gathering feathers or Ariadne
respooling thread, until the tapestry is clear.
even the loom is gone. only the clouds drifting pods
seem natural, seem to know where all of this is leading.

Notes

"Are All Your Predictions for the Future Real?" is inspired by Aimee Nezhukumatathil's poem "Are all the Break-Ups in Your Poems Real?" and an ekphrasis of a viral video of a house swept out to sea in the Outer Banks of North Carolina.

Robert Cowie's quote is taken from the article "Scientists Warn that Sixth Mass Extinction Has 'Probably Started'" published in *Vice* on January 19, 2021 by Becky Ferriera.

Toward the end of his epic poem "Metamorphosis," Ovid writes the following statement for Pythagorus: "Everything changes, nothing dies: the spirit wanders, arriving here or there, and occupying whatever body it pleases."

"Ghost Forest" was inspired by Maya Lin's exhibition of the same title, which placed 49 dead Atlantic White Cedar trees in the middle of Madison Square Park. Park goers were able to walk through the forest of 40 foot trees as a reminder of the "looming environmental calamity." When I visited in June 2020, many people were sitting and lounging and going about their everyday routine, ignoring the naked trunks around them.

"Sasquatch mourns the pygmy rabbit" started as an abecedarian from a prompt given by Rosebud Ben-Oni in her workshop "Writing Poetry of Peculiar Joys."

"Our Dreams of Late" and "Our Dreams of Love" are

inspired by the arrangement of Layli Long Soldier's poem "Obligations 2."

"The Bird Collector" is inspired by the many National Audubon Society's Lights Out volunteers who collect birds who have died from exhaustion, confusion and window strikes along the eastern coast, a migratory superhighway damaged by our cities and light pollution.

"The Hall of Forgotten Scent" is inspired by Alexandra Daisy Ginsberg's "Resurrecting the Sublime" which created a bio-synthetic scent of extinct plant species, killed off by colonial farming practices.

"Gasteranthus Extinctus" is based in part on the findings of scientists in South America found in this article from Field Museum: Lost South American wildflower named "extinctus" rediscovered (but still endangered).

"A Maladaptation of Cells" and "Avoiding Maladaptation" uses source language from the subject headings in the IPCC's Sixth Assessment Report: "Impacts, Adaptation and Vulnerability." The concrete structure of these poems along with "Chirality" and "Murmuration" would not be possible if I hadn't taken Diane Khoi Nguyen's visual poetry workshop for the 92nd Street Y in Manhattan.

"Exhibits in the Archives of Sinking and Drowning" was inspired by a New Yorker article titled "The Challenge of Making an Archive of the Climate Crisis" by Sophie Hagney. She writes, "A People's Archive of Sinking and Melting [collects objects to remember] places that may disappear because of the combined physical, political, and economic impacts of climate change." I wrote this poem in response to an activity for Jess Gigot's poetry workshop: "The Five Stages of Ecological Grief."

"We paint the baby's room with Behr's *Melting Moment*" was inspired by the actual paint names for a series of Behr paints which included Melting Moment, which was brought to my attention as a potential poem prompt by Lannie Stabile.

"Drifting Further Everyday" takes its title and inspiration from Scott Meskill's painting of the same title.

"The Earth is a Burning Haibun We Sing to Ourselves" is inspired by the title and structure of t.a. greathouse's erasure poem "Burning Haibun."

"Politicians discussing climate change" is inspired by the miniature puddle sculpture "electoral campaign" by Isaac Cordal.

"Firstborn of the Dead" is inspired by Pablo Neruda's poem "United Fruit Company."

"Living Happily at the End of the World" is inspired by Ilya Kaminsky's poem "We Lived Happily During the War."

"Tomorrow is Never" is inspired by Kay Sage's painting of the same title.

"Restoration" is inspired by Ted Kooser's poem "Abandoned Farmhouse."

The title "Exhibits in the Museum of Dust" was provided by Todd Dillard. The concept of walking through a surreal museum that this title inspired is echoed across a series of poems in this collection using a similar construction for each title.

"Sasquatch salvages the edible ruins" was inspired by comments made by Amber Sparks on twitter about the apocalypse.

"Yayoi Kusama's *Pumpkin* washed out to sea" is an ekphrasis of a YouTube video of her damaged sculpture on the coast of Japan after a typhoon.

"Sasquatch explores Fresh Kills" is based in part on the *NY Times* article "The Lessons of a Hideous Forest" by William Bryant Logan and the accompanying photographs by Damon Winter.

"Revolution" is based in part on the *NY Times* article "How Some Skinks Lost Their Legs and Then Evolved New Ones" by Veronique Greenwood.

"Rewind" is inspired by the form and structure of Todd Dillard's poem of the same title.

The series of sasquatch poems that wend their way through this collection are inspired by the metamorphoses in Jeff Vandermeer's *Southern Reach Trilogy* and *Borne* as well as Matt Bell's *Appleseed*. They are also distant cousins to Jack Bedell's series of lovely Swamp Thing poems from which they take their form as lyrical prose poems.

Acknowledgements

Jared would like to thank the editors and staff of the following journals in which poems from this collection first appeared (at times in other forms)

Acropolis Journal: "Sasquatch salvages the edible ruins"; *Contrary Magazine:* "Animal Crackers" and "The Possibility of Grief"; *The Coop:* "Yayoi Kusama's *Pumpkin* washes out to sea"; *Ctrl + V:* "Chirality," "Maladaptation of Cells," "Murmuration"; *The Dodge:* "Playing with Climate Models" *Emerge Literary Journal:* "Living Happily at the End of the World"; *Feral:* "Eruption" and "Sasquatch remembers the places he has left" as "That Would Keep You"; *Glassworks:* "Just another Tuesday in the Anthropocene"; *Ice Floe:* "Rewind"; *Identity Theory:* "Exhibits in the Museum of Dust"; *Janus Literary:* "Sasquatch Discovers an Abandoned Bunker" as "Vanitas"; *JMWW:* "Exhibits in the Archives of Sinking and Melting"; *KGB Bar Lit:* "Firstborn of the Dead," "Revolution," "The Ship of Theseus," "Tomorrow is Never" and "Watching Time Lapse Videos with My Daughter"; *Kissing Dynamite:* "The Earth is a Burning Haibun We Sing to Ourselves"; *littledeathlit:* "Sasquatch Explores Fresh Kills" as "Fresh Kills"; *Neologism:* "The feral pigs of Chernobyl are glowing"; *Night Heron Barks:* "The Bird Collector"; *Paddler's Press:* "The divers off the coast of New Florida"; *Pidgeonholes:* "Exhibits in the Museum of Ice"; *Punk Noir:* "How to smile in front of a glacier" and "Politicians discussing climate change"; *Rejection Letters:* "The Ghost Forest"; *River Mouth Review:* "Restoration"; *The Shore:* "Experiments with Time's Perception"; *Sinking City Review:* "Freediving the North

Shore Academy Barrens"; and, *Split Rock Review*: "Gasteranthus Extinctus".

Writing a book is never a solo endeavor. I would like to thank the editors at ELJ Editions for believing in this book. Ariana D. Den Bleyker has been a steadfast cheerleader of my work and put up with a lot of pestering questions from this emerging writer. I am thankful for her grace and patience. Lannie Stabile's meticulous editing and organizing of the final draft was perfect; not only was she brilliant but she made the tense process of tinkering with something I felt was "finished" as easy and fun as possible.

Thank you to my wonderful family, especially my wife Erica, who put up with me staring and typing into a screen for over a year and encouraging me to take workshops and for listening to all the ins and outs of my publishing journey. You are the best partner. I love you. I wish my grandmother was still here to hold this book. She inspired me to be creative and never stopped asking if I was going to start writing again. I started writing again, Grandma— thank you for believing in me. My beautiful, compassionate daughters are everywhere in this book. They are the reason I decided to write about climate change and to never give up hope.

Encouragements from several editors early on helped to keep me going and believe in the value of my work: thank you Shaindel Beers, Beth Gordon and Katie Manning. I could not have developed this book without the discerning eyes of a family of readers for individual poems and the early organization of the manuscript. Thank you especially to Amy Penne and Sally Badawi for somehow being able to give invaluable feedback within what seemed like minutes. My fellow *Marvelous Verses* poets, Mitch Nobis, Adrian Dallas Frandle, Nicole Tallman, Pam Yve Simon, Raegan Pietrucha, Madeleine Corley, Victoria Buitron and Joan Kwon Glass, all put up with my many random "is this a poem" messages only to later turn around and celebrate every publication and scrap of great news along the way. Thank you for being, well, Marvelous.

While many poets and artists are noted as influences for various poems in this collection, two poets stand out as mentors, friends and direct aesthetic influences on my work. Jack Bedell has answered all my poetry community questions about publishing, contracts, where to submit and who to read. His Swamp Thing poems provide a lyrical beauty and loving detail to Jack's home state. The Sasquatch here is an homage to that love and loss. Todd Dillard has been a creative force for my work, providing prompts, titles, and talking through ideas with a generosity and joy that is infectious. His surreal perceptions relating to grief as well as his loving poems to his children helped me tap into and depict the anticipatory grief found throughout these pages. I can't thank either of you enough.

Finally, if you are still reading, thank you reader. I hope this book has been able to name the mixture of hope and despair you may feel when facing the news about climate change or thinking about future generations. But please, do not stop there: find a focus point (there are so many things to address in this wide and gorgeous world) and do what you can to foster something better. Volunteer, donate, make some personal decisions and don't accept that this is over. It is not and we deserve more than our grief.

About the Author

Jared Beloff is a teacher and poet who lives in Queens, NY with his wife and two daughters. You can find his work in *Contrary Magazine, Rise Up Review, Barren Magazine, The Shore* and elsewhere. Follow him on twitter @read_instead. You can find him online at www.jaredbeloff.com.